HANDEL

Dettingen Te Deum

1743

for soprano, alto, tenor & bass soli, SATB & orchestra

Edited by Walter Emery

Order No: NOV 070125

NOVELLO

PREFACE

Handel began the Dettingen Te Deum on Sunday 17 July 1743. The date of completion is not known; but the work was more or less publicly rehearsed at the Chapel Royal on September 26, and at Whitehall Chapel on November 9 and 18; perhaps also on the 25th. The first performance, strictly speaking, was on November 27 at the Chapel Royal. No. 7 was presumably sung by Mr [Bernard] Gates, nos. 8 and 17 by Mr Abbot, as marked in the autograph score.

There were a number of performances during Handel's lifetime, but Walsh did not publish the work until 1763. This edition was corrupt; so were its immediate successors. The first text with any claim to accuracy was probably that produced by Sir George Smart for the English Handel Society in 1846-7. The German Händel-Gesellschaft edition of 1866 (Chrysander) was little better, if at all. Both Smart and Chrysander made use of the autograph score; but they appear to have had less confidence in it than it deserves. As a result, their texts include corruptions apparently derived from the Walsh edition.

Of the various sources in the British Museum, the only one that need be taken seriously is the autograph score (RM 20.h.6). This is the original composition-sketch, and is heavily corrected in places; but there is seldom any doubt about Handel's intentions.

The spelling and punctuation of the words have been modernized. When there is any doubt about the underlay, the relevant words are italicized. In no. 18, bars 118-120, Soprano II, Handel inadvertently wrote 'have I, have I trusted'. This has been corrected by analogy with bars 53 and 97.

As far as possible, editorial suggestions are indicated in the music by the usual means—square brackets, superimposed rhythmic signs, etc.

Handel's own syllable-slurs have been reproduced. The sign ⌒⊣⌒ is used to suggest slurs in parallel passages (in no. 2, compare bars 14 and 15 with 42 and 43), and sometimes to specify the underlay in places where it is unexpected.

In the accompaniment, the left-hand stave gives the continuo line, the autograph figuring, and various passages for bassoons, etc. These latter are marked, and need not be realized. The right-hand stave gives a reduction of the upper obbligato parts, for use at rehearsal or in performances with organ accompaniment. In passages accompanied by continuo alone, small notes suggest a skeleton realization. The vocal score will thus serve as a continuo part, and is intended to be so used.

Handel's use of solo voices in nos. 1 and 2 presents puzzling and probably insoluble problems. In each case, the conductor must decide what is to be done.

In no. 1 the only passage actually marked *solo* is that for alto which begins in bar 33. Its end is not marked; but presumably the *tutti* enters with the last note of bar 36. Doubts begin at bar 39, where the continuo is marked down to *p*, as at bar 33. This suggests that solo voices may have been intended in parts of bars 39-45; and it is, in fact, not difficult to work out a scheme that has some pretensions to logic. Thus:

Soprano I: solo from bar 40 to bar 45, fourth note
Soprano II: from bar 39, second note, to bar 45, first note
Alto: from bar 43 to bar 45, first note
Tenor: from bar 41 to bar 45, first note
Bass: from bar 42 to bar 45, first note

For a present-day performance, with professional soloists, the idea has its attractions. It must nevertheless be observed that in bars 39-45 the voices are almost everywhere doubled by instruments, and this may mean that Handel did not envisage soloists.

In no. 2, the alto passages in bars 10-20, and 32-38 are solos. Two questions arise. The first concerns the words 'the Father everlasting' at bars 28-32 and 56-60. In these two passages it seems likely that a bass soloist is required, since the same words are set as an alto solo at bars 16-20, and all three passages are similarly scored and marked down to *p* or even *pianiss.* Furthermore, the bass passage at bar 28 was originally doubled by bassoon, but the latter's notes were struck out; at bar 56 Handel wrote only the first note of the bassoon part, and replaced it by a rest.

The second and more difficult question concerns bars 32-44. Here the alto passage is definitely solo, as already stated; and the tenor passage (bars 38-44) corresponds so closely with the previous alto passage (bars 10-16) that it also is probably a solo. But in bars 33-38 Sopranos I and II are in unison.

A correction in the autograph at the beginning of no. 3 may throw light on this. Here the soprano line was originally marked *C I Solo* (*i.e.,* Soprano I Solo). The word *Solo* was struck out, and *tutti* inserted at bar 4, where the voice actually begins. It looks as if Handel had been thinking in terms of a female soprano soloist, but suddenly realized that his sopranos would in fact be boys. From this point onwards, the sopranos are fairly often in unison (see parts of nos. 4, 6, 7, 14, 15, 16, and 18).

If there is anything in this line of argument, one might use a female professional soloist in no. 3, and probably in bars 33-38 of no. 2 also. Here, it would seem, Handel remembered that he was writing for boys, and it might be urged that he scored the passage as he did, not because he wanted the contrast of alto solo and soprano chorus, but simply because he did not trust any solo boy to sing the passage.

The scoring of no. 11 suggests solo voices; and as Smart headed the movement *Trio*, one may suppose that by 1846 it was traditionally so treated. Smart also remarked that no. 8 was 'usually sung by a Tenor voice'.

My own opinion is that the conductor's business is to get the maximum effect out of the available resources, and that if he wishes to use soloists in the doubtful passages discussed above, he is free to do so. But the only movements that require good soloists are those marked by Handel, all for bass or baritone (nos. 7, 8, and 17). No. 11 would probably sound best if sung by a few selected members of the choir; and other 'solo' passages could be treated in the same way.

W.E.

No. 1 Chorus – WE PRAISE THEE, O GOD

18944

2

18944

8

No. 2 Chorus— ALL THE EARTH

earth doth wor-ship thee,

earth doth wor-ship thee,

earth __ doth wor-ship thee,

earth __ doth wor-ship thee,

earth doth wor-ship thee: [SOLO]* [p] the Fa - ther ev - er, ev - er -

Str. p

26

C [p]

All the earth, all the earth __ doth wor - ship thee,

[p]

All the earth, all the earth __ doth wor - ship thee,

[p] SOLO

All the earth, all the earth doth wor - ship thee,

[p] [SOLO]*

All the

last - ing.

C

32

*Bar 56. It would be reasonable to perform all these minims as crotchets; see also bar 88.

63

69

75

81

18

87

93

99

No. 3 Chorus— TO THEE ALL ANGELS CRY ALOUD

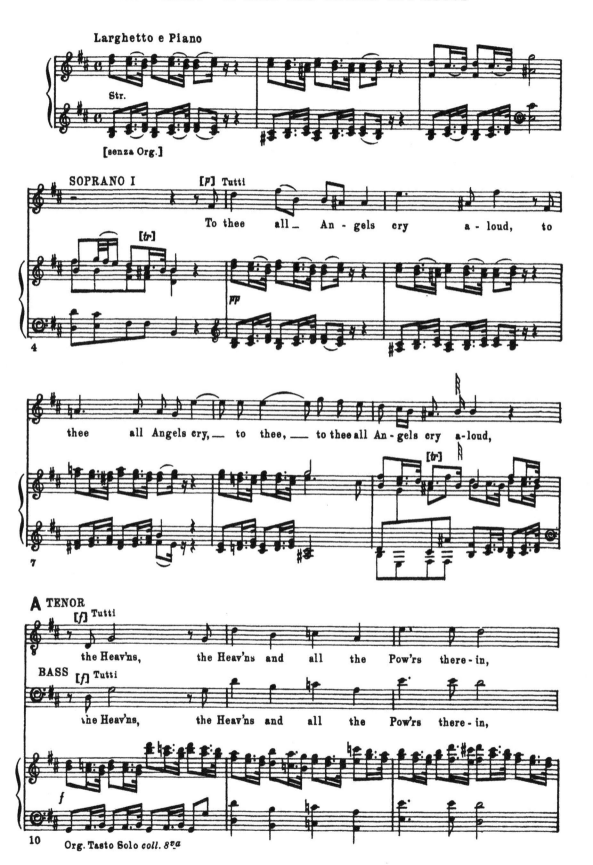

No. 4 Chorus — TO THEE CHERUBIN

thee Che - ru - bin, and Se - ra - phin con - tin - ual - ly, con - tin - ual - ly, con -

4

22

18944

B

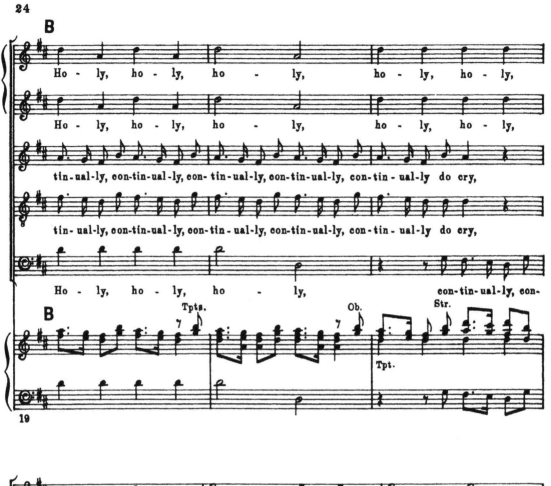

28

18944

62

69

No. 5 Chorus — THE GLORIOUS COMPANY

32

No. 6 Chorus– THINE HONOURABLE, TRUE, AND ONLY SON

No. 7 Air and Chorus — THOU ART THE KING OF GLORY

No. 8 Air – WHEN THOU TOOKEST UPON THEE

No. 9 Chorus— WHEN THOU HADST OVERCOME

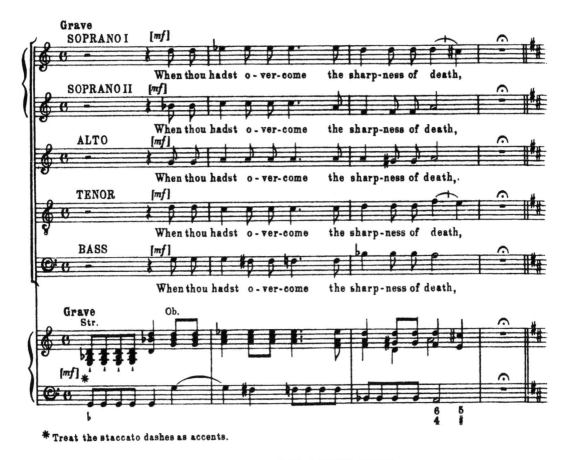

* Treat the staccato dashes as accents.

No. 10 Chorus— THOU DIDST OPEN

44

A

10

14

18944

18

21

48

No. 11 Trio* — THOU SITTEST AT THE RIGHT HAND OF GOD

* Heading. Handel did not specify solo voices.

18944

No. 12

No. 13 Chorus— WE THEREFORE PRAY THEE

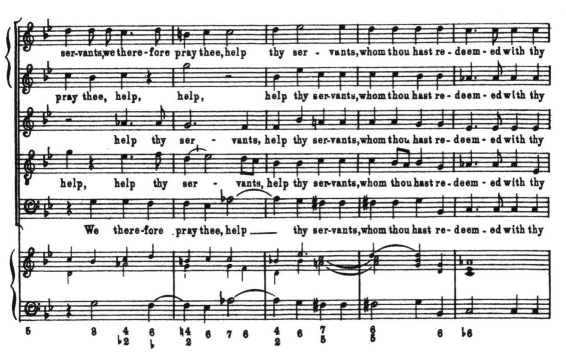

54

No. 14 Chorus— MAKE THEM TO BE NUMBERED

No. 15 Chorus— DAY BY DAY

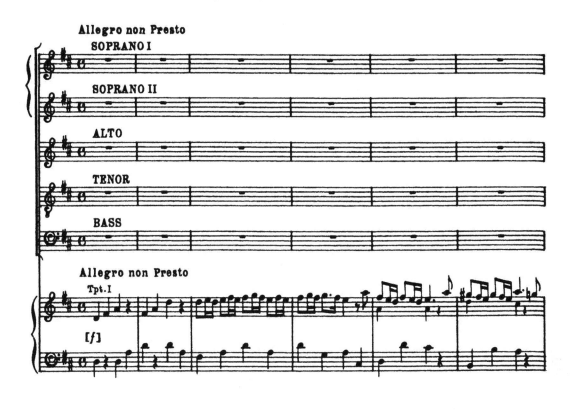

58

* Bar 15. Treat the staccato dashes as accents.

18944

24

80

No. 16 Chorus – AND WE WORSHIP THY NAME

62

18944

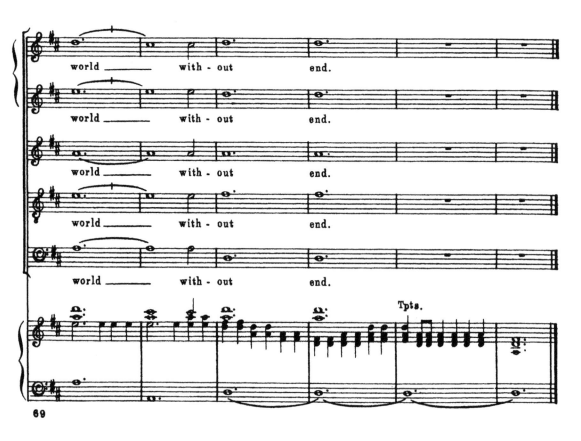

No. 17 Air— VOUCHSAFE, O LORD

light-en up-on us, as our trust is in thee, as our trust, —

12

4+
2

7 6

as our trust, our trust is in thee.

15

4+
2

4+
2

6 6 4

#

No. 18 Chorus – O LORD, IN THEE HAVE I TRUSTED

Andante

Tpts. I, II

[f]

senza Bsn.

A

col. Str. Ob.

9

col Bsn.

ALTO SOLO

B

O   Lord, in

[tr]

Ob.

Str.

*

p

16

* Bar 20. The minims are best played as crotchets.